I0151721

Emily's Secret Slippers

Written by
Veronica Gunnerson

Illustrated by
Hailey Taylor

First Edition

Casebound ISBN: 978-1-62720-412-5
Paperback ISBN: 978-1-62720-413-2

Illustrations by Hailey Taylor
Design by Sienna Whalen

Published by Apprentice House Press

Apprentice
House Press
Loyola University Maryland

Loyola University Maryland
4501 N. Charles Street, Baltimore, MD 21210
410.617.5265 • www.ApprenticeHouse.com • info@ApprenticeHouse.com

To Norman, my love and my rock still,
and to our little "Emilinky" forever.

"Emily, it's 9 o'clock. Better get up soon," Mrs. Holman called up the stairs.

Emily pulled her quilt over her head. "I don't wanna go," she murmured to Schultzie, her 4-foot brown stuffed bloodhound. Schultzie, his fur all worn and nubby, could do no more than lie there sympathetically.

Emily laid her head smack in the middle of Schultzie's back and stared out her bedroom window. She could see the top of Mrs. Lynch's willow tree, the one she'd planted last summer when Laurie was born. Everyone on the block called it Laurie's tree.

I wonder if Laurie will grow up as pretty as Ruthie, Emily thought. Ruthie was Emily's best friend.

But it was hard being best friends with the prettiest girl on the block when you were the ugliest (or thought you were, as Emily had ever since the first pimple popped out on her chin two months ago).

Ruthie's way with a baseball bat didn't help either. She could hit home runs even better than the boys. Being the tallest kid on the block, Emily was the fastest runner, though.

Ruthie would hit the ball and Emily would run to the base.
Really, she would leap to the base, 'cause that was a good way to practice ballet leaps and she didn't practice ballet very much otherwise.

"I'm only the fastest runner 'cause I have the longest legs," Emily said out loud to Schultzie. "When the other kids catch up, I won't be best at that either," she mumbled, feeling her face for any new pimples.

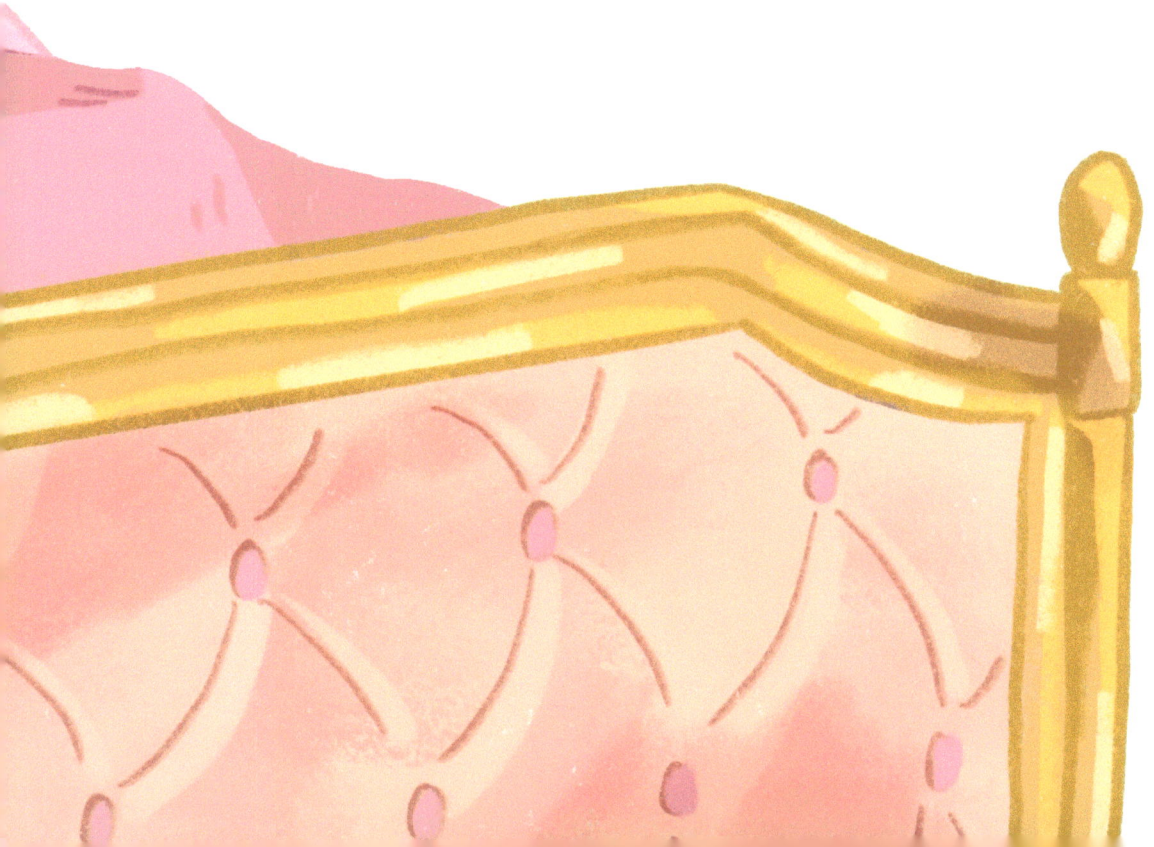

All of a sudden Mrs. Holman was standing in the doorway.

"Emily, why aren't you getting up? Don't you want to go to ballet today?" she asked.

Emily forced out a sad "Yes," so sad that Mrs. Holman didn't quite believe it.

She sat down at Emily's side, not even caring that she was wrinkling the new pink quilt.

"You don't seem to enjoy ballet anymore, honey," she said as she rubbed Emily's back the way she used to when Emily was little and wouldn't go to sleep unless Mommy rubbed her back.

"Is there something wrong?"

There was something wrong all right, thought Emily.

She had pimples, couldn't hit a lousy baseball, and worst of all,
she was the clumsiest ballerina in the whole school, if not the whole world!

"No, Mom," Emily answered. "It's just getting harder to get up early on Saturdays."

"Early!" Said Mrs. Holman, looking at her watch and laughing.

"I'd hate to hear what you call late.
Now come on downstairs for some peanut butter and bacon sandwiches
before you get dressed."

"Oh boy! Peanut butter and bacon for breakfast!" shrieked Emily, tearing out of bed.

She completely forgot how sad she was.

It wasn't until she was pulling on her black leotard over her
peanut butter-swollen tummy that Emily began feeling sad again.

"It's not that I don't like ballet," she explained to Schultzie while dressing.

"I do. It's just that it's hard to be the only one in the class who gets all mixed up."

"Come on, Emily," called Mrs. Holman. Emily buckled her sandals,
gave Schultzie a big hug and ran downstairs.

By the time Mrs. Holman pulled the yellow Volkswagen up in front of
Miss Marilyn's School of Dance, Emily was in a panic.

She wasn't thinking of the mistakes she might make, though.

She was thinking of her pink ballet slippers that were still at home in her closet.

"Mommy, I forgot my ballet slippers," Emily cried.

"I'm afraid it's too late to go back, honey," Mrs. Holman answered.

"Oh no! What'll I do?" Emily asked. She was getting hot all over.

Her face was burning the way it did last Saturday when
she did her chaîné turns right into the wall and everyone laughed, except Emily.

"Let's ask Miss Marilyn if there's an extra pair lying around," Mrs. Holman suggested.

"Can we ask her without anyone hearing?"

"I think we can," said Mrs. Holman, smiling.

"Oh yes," said Miss Marilyn when Mrs. Holman quietly told her Emily's problem.

"I'm sure we can dig up a pair somewhere."

"Thanks. See you in an hour, honey," said Mrs. Holman, waving goodbye.

To Emily's horror, Miss Marilyn then turned to the class and announced in a loud voice, "Emily's forgotten her ballet slippers. Does anyone have an extra pair?"

"She doesn't need them. She can't dance anyway," Carol Jenkins from Emily's fourth grade taunted in a not-very-low whisper.

Everyone but Emily giggled.

She's just jealous 'cause I get As in school and she doesn't, Emily told herself, blinking very hard so the tears in her eyes would stay there and not dribble down her red cheeks.

"Well, Emily," said Miss Marilyn, ignoring Carol, "if none of the girls can help, I know we have one pair of slippers you can use. Follow me."

Emily was glad to follow Miss Marilyn out of the studio
into the sunny office where Mr. Marilyn (Miss Marilyn
called him Tom) took the money from all the mothers.
Mr. Marilyn wasn't there this morning.

Thank goodness. Emily could finally relax. Her cheeks
even stopped tingling. Miss Marilyn rummaged through
the desk drawers and then through the coat closet.

"I know we have a pair somewhere," she
murmured, more to herself than to Emily.

Finally, from the darkest corner of the
wardrobe, Miss Marilyn pulled out a pair of
the oldest, dingiest, most worn-out ballet
slippers

Emily had ever seen.

"These have been here for years, Emily, since long before Tom and I took over the school. I don't know whose they were," Miss Marilyn said,

"but I'll bet they're small enough to fit you."

They were so awful that Emily hoped they wouldn't. But they slipped right on her feet as if they'd always been hers and never anyone else's.

Being very polite, Emily said, "Thank you, Miss Marilyn," and marched into the studio holding her head about as high as any 9-year-old girl could in such embarrassing circumstances.

She took her place at the ballet barre far away from Carol Jenkins.

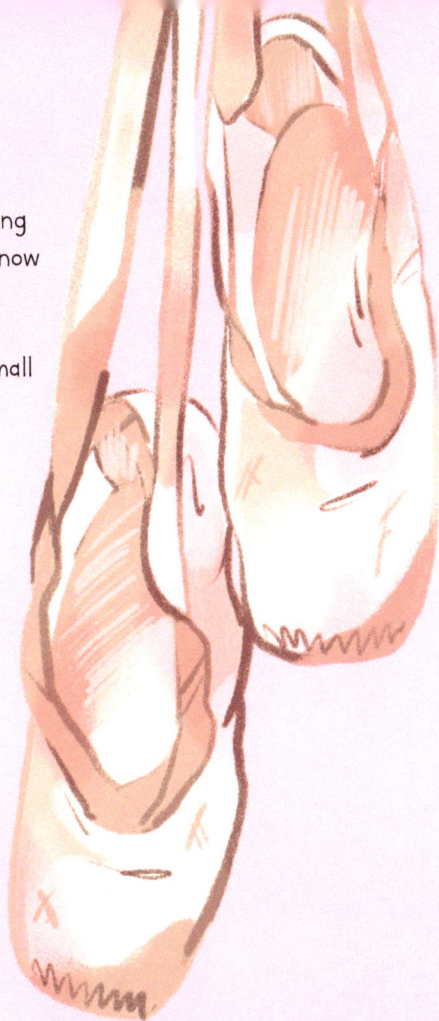

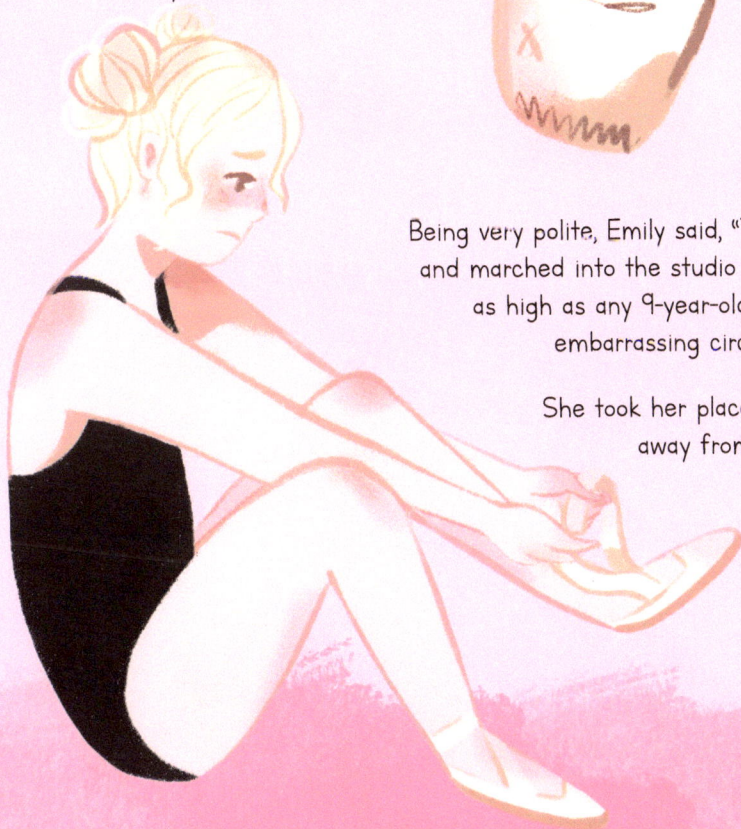

"First position," called Miss Marilyn.

Ten pairs of feet snapped together, toes pointed out.

"Second position." Toes still pointed out, ten pairs of
feet spread apart.

"Third."

"Fourth."

"Fifth."

This part was easy.

Emily always got her basic positions right.

Every time she moved her feet today, though, a tiny whiff of dust curled around her ankles.

How old can these shoes be, Emily wondered, sneaking peeks at the other girls to be sure no one was watching the dust dance around her feet.

Everyone else, even Carol Jenkins, was concentrating too hard on her own feet to bother looking at anyone else's (that was why Miss Marilyn had to yell "Heads up!" 40 times every Saturday).

"First position. Plié," called Miss Marilyn.

As Emily clicked her heels together, toes out, and bent down with her back straight as a brand-new No. 2 pencil, she let her thoughts drift away with the dust.

She imagined herself in the arms of Rudolf Nureyev, being swept across a floodlit stage the way he lovingly carried Margot Fonteyn in "Romeo and Juliet."

Mom and Dad had taken her to see it just a few weeks ago.

Maybe these slippers were hers, Emily imagined. The program didn't say where Margot lived when she was little.

Who knows?

Maybe she lived right here in this town and came to Miss Marilyn's School of Dance! She might've pliéd in these very slippers before she went off to join The Royal Ballet.

Emily was so lost in her daydream that Miss Marilyn had to say, "Emily, are you with us?" twice before Emily heard her.

When at last she did, Emily quickly pliéd. Funny how the dust settling around her feet looked more like gold dust to her now.

"All right, girls. Time to practice our chaînés."

Emily's heart started pounding the way it did whenever Daddy got mad at her.

She could even hear it in her ears. But it didn't matter. Her daydream had made her brave. There would be no wall in her face this week.

I'll do it right somehow, Emily swore to herself. She even volunteered to go first just to get it over with.

Emily walked to the corner of the room.

With her head high as a prima ballerina's and her hands clasped to her waist just so, she began.

Feet together. Turn halfway. Feet apart. On and on in a straight line she went, snapping her head around to face the far wall with every turn.

Her cheeks weren't just hot – they were on fire.

And Emily's teeth were clenched together so tight that it would've taken Mr. Holman's wrench to pry them apart.

But she did it!

Emily did chaînés perfectly all the way across the studio floor.

Carol Jenkins gaped at her. The rest of the class started clapping.

And Miss Marilyn, too surprised for words at first, finally put her hand on Emily's shoulder and said, "That was beautiful, Emily. Now that's what practice can do for all of you, girls."

(Little did Miss Marilyn know that Emily's only practice had been a few leaps to first base for Ruthie yesterday after school.)

In a daze Emily walked back to the ballet barre. She even remembered – for the first time – to step toe first as she walked, the way ballerinas do.

She could feel the whole class watching her,
but she wasn't embarrassed.

She felt like Juliet being swept across the floor
on a cloud of gold dust.

As Emily watched each girl take her turn, she began
to wonder why she ever used to get mixed up.

Chaînés were easy.

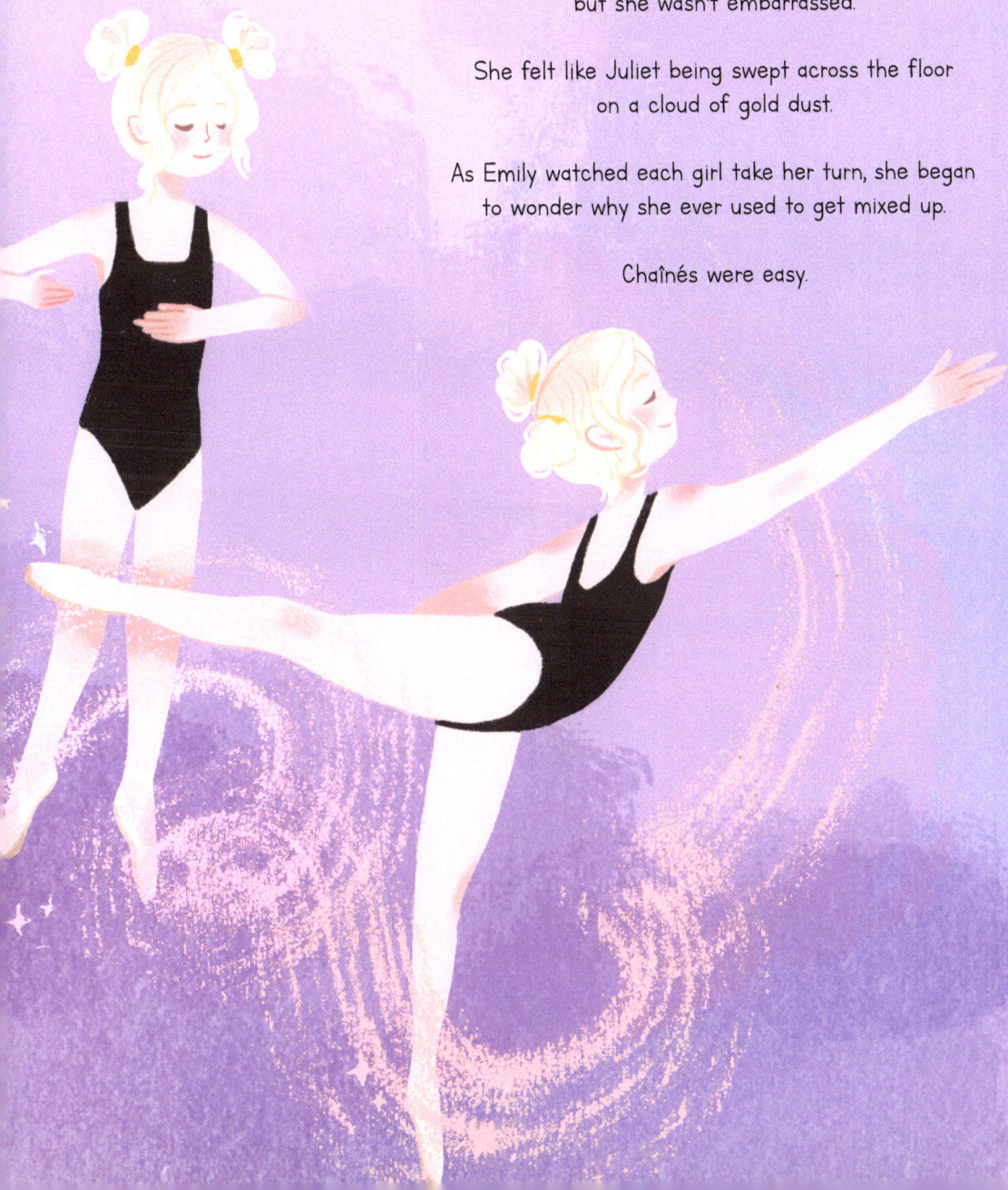

When everyone had chaînéd across the studio, Miss Marilyn made an announcement.

"This year all the ballet classes in the school will join together for the spring recital.

We're going to do 'The Nutcracker.'"

The studio burst into a chorus of shrieks and giggles and handclaps. Carol Jenkins called out, "Who gets to be Clara?"

Just as fast as it had started, all the noise stopped. Carol was the best ballerina in the 7-to-10 age group, the group from which Clara would surely be chosen.

Each little ballerina wished she could be Clara, but everyone knew who would be, unless. . . A few eyes turned to Emily, who was staring at her dusty feet.

"We won't be choosing leads for another month," Miss Marilyn answered.

"We're going to begin learning a few new steps next week, though, and from now on we'll use the music from 'The Nutcracker' as our background. See you next week."

Nine happy girls raced out of the studio screaming to their waiting parents,

"WE'RE GONNA DO 'THE NUTCRACKER'!"

Emily was the only straggler.

She was walking very slowly. . . toe, heel, toe, heel.

Mrs. Holman watched her from the doorway.

"Emily, you're doing your ballet walk. It looks so pretty. I see Miss Marilyn found shoes for you, didn't she?"

Emily simply nodded uh-huh, but a smile big as half a moon spread across her face and her eyes shone like the blue rhinestone in her bubblegum-machine ring.

"Looks like this was a good day," Mrs. Holman said to Miss Marilyn as she watched Emily tenderly remove the grungy slippers.

"It was a good day for Emily," Miss Marilyn said. "All of a sudden, she's the best ballerina in my class! She must be practicing very hard."

"If she is, she's doing it behind my back," said Mrs. Holman. They both looked at Emily a little strangely. Emily didn't notice.

She simply handed her borrowed slippers back to Miss Marilyn, said "Thank you," and then bent down to buckle her sandals.

She concentrated very hard on watching Miss Marilyn out of the corner of her eye, though, so hard that it made her head hurt.

As soon as she saw where Miss Marilyn put the worn ballet slippers, Emily was ready to go.

When she got home, the kids were playing baseball in the street.

Ruthie came running over.

"How was ballet?" she asked.

"It was wonderful, Ruthie," Emily answered.

"It was?"

"I was the best one!"

"You were?"

"Uh-huh. Honest."

"Wow! You wanna try to bat today?"

"No. I'll just run for you some more. It's good practice," said Emily.

"Okay," said Ruthie, figuring her best friend knew what she was talking about.

The next Saturday Emily was up and ready for ballet before her mother
had even poured the orange juice.

She was too worried to eat but forced down some Cheerios so her mother
wouldn't ask, "What's wrong?"

"Don't forget your ballet slippers today, Emily," Mrs. Holman said as she cleared the table.

"I won't, Mom," said Emily.

And she didn't.

But when she got to Miss Marilyn's, she stayed behind in the waiting room,
her heart beating harder every second, until everyone had filed into the studio.

Then, faster than Schultzie would be if he were real,
Emily ran to the wardrobe and pulled open the door.

There, right in front where Miss Marilyn had dumped them, were the dusty old ballet slippers.

Emily quickly traded hers for them and ran into the studio.

Miss Marilyn was just calling up "The Nutcracker" from her playlist.
They weren't even going to practice basic positions today!

They were going to learn new steps right away.

Emily looked down hopefully. No gold dust this week.

Last week's lesson had shaken all the dust off the worn slippers.
Emily paid very close attention anyway, just in case.

She listened to every word and watched Miss Marilyn do the steps to
the Children's Galop from "The Nutcracker."

It wasn't very easy.

Even Carol Jenkins had a little trouble learning the new steps right away.

Emily's turn was last.

There being nothing else to cross since ballerinas use their fingers, toes, arms and legs, Emily crossed her eyes for good luck.

Then she started dancing.

When she stopped, even Carol Jenkins clapped.

No one knew how it had happened (no one but Emily, that is), but Emily really was the best ballerina in the 7- to 10-year-old class.

Just before class ended, Emily mumbled, "Have to go to the bathroom," and darted out of the studio faster than Peter Rabbit with Mr. McGregor on his heels.

She made her slipper switch a second before Miss Marilyn came through the door.

From then on, Emily never missed a switch.

Her secret slippers were more important to her than even Schultzie, though of course she would never forget his kind understanding.

She knew he was just as proud of her as Mom and Dad and Ruthie were when Miss Marilyn picked her to be Clara.

Emily practiced hard these days, even though she had her secret slippers. She was afraid if she didn't, her parents would start suspecting something.

On the Saturday before dress rehearsal, Emily skipped into Miss Marilyn's School early as she always did now to make her slipper switch. She pulled open the wardrobe door and bent down to pick up her secret slippers.

They weren't there.

Emily froze. She stared at the wardrobe floor, not even knowing what to do next.
She felt all over the floor. She crawled inside and examined every corner.

Her slippers were gone. Just then Miss Marilyn walked in.
"What are you doing, Emily?" she asked.

Emily jumped up and out of the wardrobe.
"Remember those old slippers I used once?" she asked quickly.

"Yes! After you forgot yours, Emily, I realized how important it is for the school to have some extra ballet shoes around. I've been buying one pair at a time in each size ever since. This week I finally replaced those old ones."

"Replaced?" said Emily in a sick little voice.

"Yes. We threw away those poor, beat-up slippers. They were of no use anymore, Emily, though I'm certainly glad they were here the day you needed them.

Do you need an extra pair today?"

"No, thank you," said Emily. Her heart was breaking as she put on her own pink ballet slippers.

She couldn't be Clara now.

She probably wouldn't even be good enough to be an extra kid in the Children's Galop.

"Come on then, Emily," Miss Marilyn said. "Can't dawdle this week. It's the last class before dress rehearsal."

Last class before dress rehearsal? That's right, thought Emily.

There won't be a recital if there's no Clara. I have to do it.

Emily had never been so scared in her whole life. She watched Miss Marilyn tap on "The Nutcracker" on her playlist.

"We'll practice the Children's Galop first," Miss Marilyn said.

Emily walked, toe first, to her place on the other side of the studio.

It was supposed to be Christmas Eve in Dr. Stahlbaum's home in Germany. Emily wished it were Christmas Eve in her own home and she were safely snuggled in bed with Schultzie.

The music began.
All eyes were on Emily.
She was leader of the Galop.
But Emily didn't move.

"Emily, it's time," whispered Carol Jenkins.

"Emily?" Miss Marilyn said. She stopped the music. "Are you all right?"

Emily swallowed hard. "Yes, Miss Marilyn," she said softly.

"Well, let's try again then," said Miss Marilyn.

Miss Marilyn tapped the screen on her iPad once again.

Emily took a deep breath, crossed her eyes for good luck and began dancing when she heard the music start again.

Emily danced and danced. She didn't know if she was doing anything right, but she was too frightened to stop. If only I had my slippers, she cried inside.

Finally, the music stopped. Emily stopped.

She waited.

She knew Miss Marilyn would have to turn over the lead to Carol Jenkins. Tears came to her eyes. How would she tell Mom and Dad and Ruthie? They were all so proud of her.

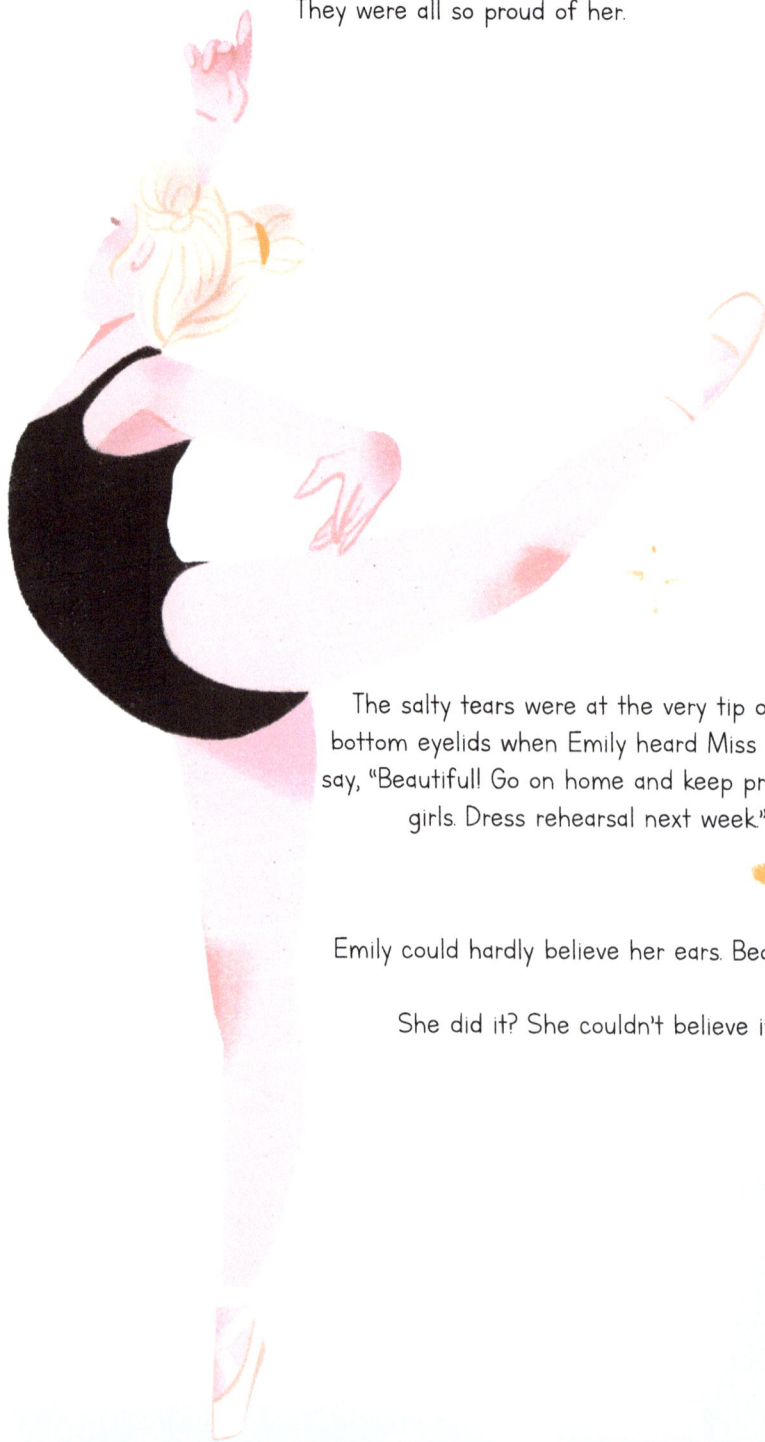

The salty tears were at the very tip of her bottom eyelids when Emily heard Miss Marilyn say, "Beautiful! Go on home and keep practicing, girls. Dress rehearsal next week."

Emily could hardly believe her ears. Beautiful?

She did it? She couldn't believe it.

Still on the brink of tears, she looked down so
no one would see how wet her eyes were.

And when she did, she got another surprise.

There on the floor dancing around her feet

Emily could see a tiny
whiff of dust – gold dust.

Ronnie Gunnerson – Author

Veronica "Ronnie" Gunnerson retired in 2021 after a career in communications – first as a business journalist in the early days of the personal computer and home video industries, then as a public relations executive at Turner Broadcasting System, Inc. (now Warner Bros. Discovery), and finally as an affiliate associate professor at Loyola University Maryland. "Emily's Secret Slippers" marks the beginning of the fourth phase of her communications journey. Widowed with grown children and grandchildren, her Calico Cat Minnie and Yorkshire Terrier Nellie keep her company as she sits at her desk looking out at the Chester River on Maryland's Eastern Shore finally pursuing the life she always dreamed of – that of a full-time writer.

Hailey Taylor, Illustrator

Hailey Taylor has a BFA in Illustration from the Maryland Institute College of Art (MICA). She specializes in creating whimsically narrative and character-focused art. Hailey loves working with a variety of different media, including gouache, acrylic, digital, and even rug tufting. In March 2017, Hailey took her passion for art and animals and created a cat cafe called Kittens In Cups. By partnering with her local shelter, the AACSPCA, they have placed over 400+ cats in happy homes! She actively uses her passion for animals and art to enrich her community.

Acknowledgments

I am indebted to Dr. Kevin Atticks, publisher of Apprentice House, for his enthusiasm, support and willingness to accept my first book for publication. Sincere thanks to Natalie Misyak and Sienna Whalen for their exquisite attention to detail in the overall design and editing of my work. I will forever hold Hailey Taylor in my heart with the deepest admiration and gratitude for the amazing job she did illustrating the story of an insecure little girl who learns to believe in herself. Finally, I would like to thank my dad, Raymond Fannon, who died when I was 11 but not before making sure I knew how much he believed in my own little dreams, and my deceased husband, Norman, without whose constant support I would never have achieved any of those little dreams.

Apprentice
House Press
Loyola University Maryland

Apprentice House is the country's only campus-based, student-staffed book publishing company. Directed by professors and industry professionals, it is a nonprofit activity of the Communication Department at Loyola University Maryland.

Using state-of-the-art technology and an experiential learning model of education, Apprentice House publishes books in untraditional ways. This dual responsibility as publishers and educators creates an unprecedented collaborative environment among faculty and students, while teaching tomorrow's editors, designers, and marketers.

Outside of class, progress on book projects is carried forth by the AH Book Publishing Club, a co-curricular campus organization supported by Loyola University Maryland's Office of Student Activities.

Eclectic and provocative, Apprentice House titles intend to entertain as well as spark dialogue on a variety of topics. Financial contributions to sustain the press's work are welcomed. Contributions are tax deductible to the fullest extent allowed by the IRS.

To learn more about Apprentice House books or to obtain submission guidelines, please visit www.apprenticehouse.com.

Apprentice House
Communication Department
Loyola University Maryland
4501 N. Charles Street
Baltimore, MD 21210
410-617-5265
info@apprenticehouse.com
www.apprenticehouse.com

www.ingramcontent.com/pod-product-compliance
Lightning Source LLC
Chambersburg PA
CBHW040916100426

42737CB00042B/98